BUYING A
COMPUTER

BUYING A
COMPUTER

CONSUMERS' ASSOCIATION

Which? Books are commissioned and researched by
Consumers' Association and published by
Which? Ltd,
2 Marylebone Road, London NW1 4DF
Email address: books@which.net

Distributed by The Penguin Group:
Penguin Books Ltd, 27 Wrights Lane, London W8 5TZ

First edition October 1997
Copyright © 1997 Which? Ltd

British Library Cataloguing in Publication Data
A catalogue record for this book is available from the British
Library

ISBN 0 85202 688 9

Buying a Computer contains information from *The Which? Guide
to Computers* by Richard Wentk

> For a full list of Which? books, please write to Which? Books,
> Castlemead, Gascoyne Way, Hertford X, SG14 1LH
> or access our website at http://www.which.net

Cartoons and cover illustration by David Pattison, Cartoon
Partnership
Cover design by Creation Communications
Typeset by Saxon Graphics Ltd, Derby
Printed and bound in Great Britain by Caledonian International
Book Manufacturers, Glasgow

CONTENTS

CONTENTS

INTRODUCTION

A computer is the perfect tool for manipulating information. In the office it can replace the ageing typewriter, act as a very fast adding machine and provide easy access to the books and other records. In the home it can be used for writing letters, entertaining and educating children, playing games and managing personal finances.

However, any modern machine, even a modest one, can be used for much more than these tasks. In fact, a computer can be used to help with almost anything, from automating a bakery to keeping track of stock in a shop or displaying examples of different hairstyles to customers with their own features superimposed electronically.

The term 'information' can cover words, sounds, photographs and numbers. Even images such as maps and technical drawings can be stored and manipulated on most modern computers. New uses, such as photographic editing and retouching, interior design and automated route-planning are beginning to appear in sophisticated forms.

A computer is a sizeable investment. Used wisely, it can streamline the running of any business. Unfortunately, it can also become more of a problem than a solution. It is possible to cripple a business by making the wrong decision in purchasing and using a computer system.

WHAT DO YOU WANT YOUR COMPUTER FOR? [1]

When you are choosing a computer system, it is important to approach things from the perspective of tasks, then software, then hardware. You have tasks that need to be carried out. A computer may be able to help you with them if you have the right software. So take a look at the software available and decide which package you might find useful for which tasks:

- word-processing
- desktop publishing and design
- bookkeeping
- databases
- spreadsheets
- Internet
- leisure uses.

Word-processing

Why use a word-processor when a typewriter will do? If you have been using a typewriter for many years without problems, why pay the extra for a word-processing system? For some kinds of work a typewriter is still perfectly adequate: a cheap, reliable way to produce high-quality letters. For something more versatile, however, it is worth considering a computer-based word-processing system.

8

The chief advantage of electronic systems is that you can correct mistakes before you print them. You can make as many changes as you like in a document before the print touches the paper. Paragraphs are managed automatically. If you delete a word in a sentence the remaining words move to fill in the gap.

Word-processing also gives a range of broader editing options. Words, sentences and paragraphs can be moved around. Text can be copied from one document to another. Footnotes and headers can be added and pages can be numbered automatically. You can also keep electronic copies of your work, so that letters can be stored inside the computer or on floppy discs and re-used later with minor changes. It is also possible to build up a library of blank letterheads addressed to different people, which can save typing in their details every time.

A very useful word-processor feature which has been available for some time is the mail merge facility. Mail merge works by taking a standard letter and then filling in the details from a separate list. It can also be used to print envelopes.

Desktop publishing and design

Whereas word-processing is text-oriented and ideal for letters, memos and faxes, desktop publishing (DTP) is used whenever text and graphics have to be laid out on a page. Typical uses include newsletters, price lists, advertising flyers and posters.

DTP continues where top-end word–processors leave off, by adding features such as the ability to split text between columns and pages, to make it flow around complicated shapes, to print it upside-down, sideways, at an angle or along a curved line, and to include photographs and other images on the page. Font-handling makes it easy to produce banner headlines, paragraph headings and quote boxes. Lines, ovals, boxes and frames can be added to draw attention to areas of text, and textures and borders can be created to make a document look more ornate. Unlike word-processing software, which is almost exclusively used to print letters in black on white paper, all but the very cheapest DTP software can work with colour, although you will need access to a colour printer to print it out in colour.

10

Even a budget DTP package is capable of far more striking results than a word-processor. The two are often used together, with the latter providing basic text-editing features and the former more sophisticated page layout facilities. Most DTP software can import text directly from a range of popular word-processing packages. This ensures that special effects such as italics are maintained.

Graphics can be imported in a similar way. These can be clip art or graphs or tables that have been created using other software. (Clip art is a selection of basic cartoons, images, drawings and sketches, often supplied as part of a DTP package. As with fonts, extra images are available at additional cost.)

Bookkeeping

For most businesses keeping the books is something of a chore. A computer can automate the work, as well as producing professional end-of-year accounts. VAT calculations can also be made much less time-consuming. It is relatively simple to automate VAT accounting, including any rate changes and zero-rated items. It is also possible to produce a single printout at the end of the accounting period which can be sent straight to HM Customs and Excise with a covering letter.

Sole traders can use a computer to keep track of their creditors and debtors. This can be combined with invoice- and cheque-printing systems, to provide an all-in-one cash flow control system. It is possible to set up a system whereby bad debts are chased with letters, as well as making sure that bills are paid as late as possible to help with cash flow. One advantage of a system like this is that it enables you to estimate accurately the financial position of your business a month or two ahead, based on sales projections.

Advanced accounting systems can handle credits and debits in foreign currencies, and allow for exchange-rate fluctuations. The job of calculating payroll contributions is also relatively straightforward. The computer can be made to allow for budget and tax changes and even refer to them on a year-by-year basis. Keeping track of payroll outgoings, PAYE and National Insurance contributions becomes much simpler.

Databases

Databases are used to organise information in a user-defined way. They are powerful complex programs which can be used to extract summaries of information as well as keeping it together. Databases are completely open-ended, so you can organise your information in any way you like. You can also filter the information in different ways by presenting the database with a query. This produces a broad picture, known as a report, which conveniently summarises the facts and can help you spot trends, anomalies and other patterns. If, for example, you are maintaining a list of sales, you can create a report which totals the sales you have made to each customer. You could also total sales by geographical area, by specific towns, or even from all customers whose surnames begin with 'W'. It is this flexibility that makes databases so powerful and useful.

There are two kinds of database: flatfile databases store information in a single table, and are the computer equivalent of a card index. The 'cards' can be very complicated, with hundreds of entries on each one, but each card uses the same template for the information.

Relational databases spread information across different tables, while maintaining links between them, so you do not need to copy information unnecessarily. To understand this better, imagine a series of orders, each of which includes a customer's name and address. A flatfile database would require you to type in the name and address for every single order received from that customer. With a relational database you can assign each customer a number or code instead. The customer's details are kept in one place, and the order details make a reference to them. If the customer moves, you only have to type in the new address once. This is obviously quicker and more likely to be accurate than retyping the same information every time.

An important feature to look for when choosing a database is referential integrity. This means the software ensures that you never enter information without all the details filled in (for example, you cannot create a purchase order without a set of customer details to go with it). Not all databases check for this, and without this feature you can experience problems as links between different kinds of information become confused.

13

Relational databases can be used for much more than maintaining names and addresses and keeping track of sales.

Spreadsheets

A spreadsheet is a general-purpose calculation tool. It provides a grid of cells that you can fill with information: a number, a date, a word or a formula. Most cells contain a number but they can also contain a formula that works with the numbers – a total, an average, a percentage and so on. The formulas can be simple or complex. Many spreadsheets are used as adding machines, providing a total for a set of figures in a column and then a grand total for the row of subtotals across the bottom. The range of possibilities is huge, however, and covers everything from simple arithmetic to complicated financial calculations such as loan repayment schedules, pricing based on profit margins, and useful figures such as the internal rate of return. Some spreadsheets include formulas to help with statistical analysis and engineering, and can handle general mathematical problems such as matrix manipulations and equation-solving.

The biggest advantage of a spreadsheet is the ease with which it can re-calculate results. If one entry is changed in a column, the total at the bottom changes.

If you decide you need a spreadsheet, it is a good idea to look first at those included as part of an 'office suite'. These all-in-one packages include a spreadsheet, word-processor, database and other optional extras such as presentation software and perhaps a personal information manager or a contact manager. A suite-based spreadsheet gives you integration between these different programs, so that information can be exchanged between them all quickly and easily.

Many spreadsheets can present information graphically. Pie charts, bar charts, line graphs and maps are all common. So, for example, you could prepare the financial aspects of a business plan in a spreadsheet, and then transfer the graphs and tables over to a word-processor or DTP package to present them professionally.

The Internet

To access the Internet you need a telephone and a modem. You can then open an account with an Internet service provider to gain access to the Internet. You pay for this in much the same way that you pay for your existing telephone line, with a monthly subscription. Usually access is via your modem over a telephone link – your computer dials the provider's computer, and a connection between the two is made. What happens next depends on the kind of service your provider offers. Some act as an electronic *poste restante*, collecting mail and other information for you, holding it until you dial in and then forwarding it to you along the telephone lines. Others act as a gateway that connects your computer directly to the Internet. This kind of connection is much more useful, but it can also be harder to set up and use. However, it is not necessarily any more expensive, and once it is up and running it can give you many more options and much better access to the services that the Internet offers.

Access to the Internet offers a number of useful services:

- **Electronic mail** (email) Messages can be passed from computer to computer directly. Unlike network email, however, the computers can be anywhere in the world.
- **Free access to software and other information** A large number of software archives around the world offer unlimited free access to thousands of shareware and freeware software packages. Other kinds of information, such as current weather satellite images, recipes, travel information and hints and tips for almost every sport and hobby, are also widely available.
- **Free access to services which can help you find this information** Knowing that the information is available is only part of the story. With the total number of computers on the Internet in the millions, it can be impossible to track down what you want without help. A number of free services (with colourful names like Gopher and Veronica) make this easier. These are fast, 'intelligent' search tools that scan the Internet looking for information on a keyword basis.
- **Newsgroups** These are public discussion areas. There are over 10,000 groups available and the numbers are increasing every day. They are arranged

according to subject matter, which includes everything from computer topics to poodle-breeding and music fan clubs. Most service providers supply only a selection of the more popular and useful English-language groups. The computer-oriented groups – and there are many – are a good place to find free support.

- **The World Wide Web (WWW)** Part magazine, part art form, part encyclopedia, the World Wide Web is a global hypertext system. Pages of text and pictures contain highlighted words which link to relevant information stored elsewhere either as part of the same document or part of a different document on another computer in a different country. The most useful thing the WWW can offer the user is international advertising space. Many organisations and individuals now have their own web 'pages' and it is an excellent way to reach millions of potential customers.

- **News wire services** These offer direct access to Reuters, Associated Press and other news agencies. A number of electronic newspapers (such as Clarinet) are also available. For the most part, the cost of these services is in addition to the normal Internet connection. The advantage of subscribing is that you get the news as soon as it happens. Several news-filtering services, the equivalent of press-cutting agencies, are starting to become available.

Leisure uses

Since the late 1980s the home computer has gradually been integrated with other home entertainment

17

and leisure products. A plug-in extra called a TV tuner is now available which transforms a computer into a television set. Many computers can now play music compact discs (CDs) through a pair of attached speakers. The same CD player can also be used to view videos, which are also supplied in CD form. Software is also being supplied on special CDs called CD-ROMs (compact discs with read-only memory). These look like ordinary music CDs but contain information instead of music. CD-ROMs have a vast storage capacity, and new kinds of multimedia software (which includes pictures, sounds and video clips as well as words) have been developed to take advantage of this.

Other leisure uses include art and music. With all creative applications the power of the computer is demonstrated in the ease with which beginners can correct mistakes. A musician can record a performance and then correct individual notes. The corrections can be as obvious as changing wrong notes, or as subtle as tiny changes in phrasing or rhythm. An artist can remove the last brush stroke, rub out sections of a picture without leaving any traces, or change the colours after a picture is finished.

There is also a small but growing market in educational software. These applications range from simple counting and reading games for pre-school and primary school children, to more advanced 'adventures' in science. Some of these have obvious uses as a worthwhile and educational distraction for children whose harassed parents would like a break. A number of educational and general-interest titles are

18

aimed at adults: for example, various encyclopedias are now available in CD-ROM format. Unlike a paper encyclopedia these include snatches of sound, music and video to enhance the presentation of information.

Finally there are computer games. These are developing into an art form in their own right, and the latest games are now designed and created by the same studios that produce Hollywood films.

IS A COMPUTER ESSENTIAL?

Every year the computer industry spends millions of pounds in the attempt to persuade people to buy its products. For all this, you may find you do not need a computer at all.

It is tempting to buy a computer 'just because'. If you look at your needs closely, however, you may decide that you do not need one at all. If you have less than £500 to spend and intend to use your computer mainly for writing letters, then it may be better to look at some of the all-in-one word-processors currently available. These cost between £200 and £400, and offer you many of the features of a computer-based system. They have the advantage of being easier to use, easier to move from one place to another and easier to learn.

Buying second-hand

If you want to dabble in the basics of computing, but are not concerned about doing any serious work or keeping up with the very latest developments, then consider a second-hand machine. These are adequate for light-duty work, will introduce you to all the basic concepts and can cost as little as £100. They will not be able to work with the latest software and hardware, so you should assume that you are buying a closed system. In other words, what you buy is what you get. Extras are not an option. For someone on a strict budget they can prove an excellent, low-risk introductory purchase.

No need to spend a fortune

If you are planning to use your computer for more business-oriented tasks, you can expect to pay £500 for a basic modern machine to over £10,000 for a no-expense-spared system. In general, you get the best compromise between cost and performance at around £1,500, for a complete system including printer and software. This will give you a modern machine that you can expand as your funds grow, but which will have a life of at least three or four years. (At the end of that period it will still be useful, but you will need to re-assess your needs in light of techno-logical advances.)

Tasks better done by hand

When it comes to looking at the individual facets of your business, the best approach to computerisation is to ask yourself how much time you spend on certain activities and how organised you are already. If you are perfectly happy keeping addresses and phone num-

20

bers in a card file, then you should think long and hard before buying an electronic system to replace them. In general, activities that you perform occasionally are best done by hand. Activities that are time-consuming, repetitive and a chore are best done by computer, but if you have a system that works for you now without a computer, there is no good reason why you should feel any need to buy one.

How much time and money would a computer actually save you?

As a rough guide you can start by working out how much time you waste over the course of a year on tasks that add nothing to the value of your business. Next, calculate how much this time is worth at a suitable hourly rate. Estimate how much time these activities will take if you get a computer to help you. For some kinds of work – VAT, payroll calculations and so on – this should be relatively straightforward. You can guesstimate how long it would take to type the relevant information into the computer, and then add a week or so as 'learning time'. Other kinds of work will be much harder to quantify and you may need to arrange a demonstration at a reputable computer store before you can get an idea. Once this is done, you can work out the time- and cost-saving of installing a computer by comparing these two figures.

This will only be a rough guide; the installation of a computer sometimes results in improved productivity

21

and new business opportunities which are not always foreseeable. By doing this comparison, you will at least have some idea of whether you are buying on a whim or taking a calculated risk.

Buying Options 2

To get the most from a computer you need to remember that you are not just buying a collection of gadgets and widgets, but a complete system – something that is very much greater than the sum of its parts. Computer advertising often tries to lure novice users into spending more than they need by tempting them with vague promises of speed and power. In practice, these factors can have surprisingly little to do with long-term usefulness and reliability. Buying the fastest computer in the world is a waste of time and money if you spend all your time struggling with it. Similarly, a computer that breaks down or leaves you baffled can be more of a liability than an asset.

Initial Considerations

It is important to leave the glossy advertising to one side and look realistically at the different elements of a computer system.

Hardware

Hardware is the physical parts of the computer – keyboard, screen, main system unit and any other extras you decide to buy. Think of it as an extension to your office. Inside the computer's case you will find the equivalent of a filing cabinet for storing information and a desk-like area where you can choose from a selection of useful tools. The more you spend on hardware the more quickly these tools will do their work for you, and the more room there will be in your new 'office' for both tools and information. There are many different kinds of computer but the two most popular lines are the IBM-compatible PC (known as the PC) and the Apple Macintosh (known as the Mac).

Software

Software is the tools or programs which run on the hardware and more often than not you will need to buy them separately. There are hundreds, perhaps even thousands, of different kinds of software available today, all tailor-made to help you with specific kinds of work. For example, if you want to write letters or create text you need word-processing software; to keep track of finances, you buy an accounting package.

Software, much more than hardware, determines how productive your computer will be. Good software is so easy to use that you forget that it is there. It is also easy to learn (user-friendly), which means you can start doing useful work with it very quickly. Bad software can be a hindrance, forcing you to work around it rather than work with it. It can also cause difficulties when you start to use it: for example, when your computer does something unexpected and you are left floundering and confused with no idea what to do next.

'Choose your software first' is one of the golden rules of computer-buying. Work out what you want to do, decide which software will work best, and then find the hardware to match.

The hardware and software are the most obvious parts of a computer system, but there are a number of other options you also need to consider.

Support

Support means help with maintenance and problem-solving. If you rely on your computer on a daily basis you need to be sure that the support will be efficient and quick – being left without your computer for a week or a month can be disastrous.

The other kind of support is needed for those times when you are unable to work out what to do next. You may perhaps be using a word-processor that claims you can print lettering in italics, but even though you have looked at the instruction manual you still can't see how to do this. At times like these it is a very good idea to have someone or something you can refer to – otherwise you can find yourself wasting a lot of time or using your software at a tiny fraction of its potential.

Training

Training is closely related to support and provides you with the help you need to get started. There are numerous training resources available, some very affordable. Courses or personal tuition can prove expensive, so you may want to consider books, videos and computer-based training software. Magazines can also be a supplementary source of introductory hints and tips.

Insurance

This is vital to ensure that if something goes wrong, you have the financial resources to put it right. If your computer fails or is stolen you may be left without access to the information essential to the running of your business. In the short term such a loss can be crippling; in the long term it can be catastrophic. Fortunately, you can protect yourself from these kinds of risks. You can insure your system to protect the information as well as the system itself. You can also keep the information safe by making regular safety copies or backups.

Security

Security becomes an issue when your information is confidential, or you are not the only person with access to it. You should be aware of the legal considerations if you start to collect information about your customers or your employees. There are ways to protect information and ensure that it can be read only by selected users.

The other kind of security is much simpler and cruder – you need to protect your computer against theft. This is a growing problem, especially in large towns and cities. Again, basic steps can be taken to make sure that your equipment is as unattractive to thieves as possible.

THE BUYING PROCESS

Once you have decided what you need and looked at the options, you can start the buying process. Don't rush into it, however. There are good ways and bad ways to buy a computer. Briefly, you are likely to have the following options:

- hire a consultant
- buy a complete package from a dealer or by mail-order
- do the research and buying yourself
- buy a second-hand system
- ask a computer-literate friend or colleague to guide you through the process.

Hiring a consultant

Hiring a consultant is by far the easiest and the least time-consuming way to buy a computer. It should also – in theory, at least – give you the best results. Unfortunately, in the short term it is by far the most expensive approach.

Consultancy fees can vary from £25 to £250 an hour; the rate depends on the consultant's experience and the size of project. Computerising a sole trader's business is relatively straightforward. Computerising a medium-sized company which has offices in different parts of the country requires a much higher level of expertise.

It is prudent to discuss exactly what the terms of your working relationship will be and, if possible, draw up a full contract so that if there are any problems you are covered legally, and both of you know exactly where you stand.

Although a consultant can be expensive – perhaps doubling the price of your computer system – the long-term benefits could justify the initial outlay. If your computer is vital to the efficient running of your business and you are unsure of your own technical abilities then a consultant can be a very cost-effective option.

Buying from a dealer

Buying from a dealer can be a risk. Computer dealers range from small shops run by enthusiasts to large multinational companies. They also vary widely in terms of quality of service, reliability, professionalism and support. The ideal is a friendly local dealer who has a strong interest in retaining your business, enjoys working in the trade and has plenty of experience to draw on.

Unfortunately, some dealers are less than scrupulous. If you fall foul of one of these you can find yourself being deliberately misled by someone who wants to off-load obsolete stock at an inflated price and has no interest in your needs or long-term custom.

Finding a trustworthy dealer

To ascertain whether you are dealing with a saint or a shark simply visit your local dealer in person, explain roughly what you are looking for and listen closely to the response. Vague sales pitches such as 'This is the very best', 'Everybody uses this one' or 'Really fast machines, these' should be treated with suspicion. You

should ask yourself a number of questions regarding the dealer. Does there seem to be a genuine understanding of what your needs are? Is there a wide range of options to choose from, or are you being steered towards stock that is piled high in the shop front? Does the shop assistant demonstrate knowledge of the subject and a professional attitude? If you feel confident about the level of aptitude and service then you have probably found your source. You may pay more in the beginning this way, but you may also find yourself with a free source of help and advice – both of which can be invaluable for inexperienced users.

If you are unable to find a good local dealer, you have the option of buying by mail-order from computer magazines. You cannot realistically expect the same level of service from a mail-order dealer –

especially a large one – as you would from a small local shop.

High-street retailers

It is tacitly acknowledged in the industry that high-street retailers of electronic products are likely to offer you the worst of both worlds. Prices are often significantly higher than elsewhere, and the level of support and help that the staff can offer tends to be minimal. At best you may be steered towards big-name products that happen to be in stock at the time. At worst you may find that you know more about the computers than the staff. Some high-street retailers offer telephone support – at a price. If you want help – and you will need it if you are new to computers – you will probably be asked to pay for it by the minute on an 0891 number. This can be stressful and expensive, and you have no guarantee that your problem will be solved.

High-street stores often charge a much higher annual percentage rate (APR) than a bank or other credit source might. As a result, you can find yourself spending the kind of sums that might have bought you the services of a consultant, yet you could still be left with something that you cannot use properly, which does not quite do the job you want, and which you do not understand.

Doing it yourself

Doing the background research and buying a computer yourself is the most time-consuming option and the most demanding in terms of your personal resources.

Buying a computer 'blind' with no research at all is very unlikely to get you a good deal. In fact, it may not even get you something you can use effectively.

If you have the time, it can be worth learning the basics of the subject from the hundreds of books, magazines and courses that are available. This can be a good investment as dealers tend to respect knowledgeable customers more than complete novices.

This approach can only be recommended if you are not in a hurry, if your computer is not going to be central to the running of your business and if you feel you have the abilities to take on the subject in depth. The rewards can be high, however. You will be able to save on hardware costs, because you will know how and what to buy and at a much lower price. You will also be less dependent on outside help. The disadvantage is that it takes time to learn all you need to know to reach this standard.

Buying second-hand

At first sight, the second-hand approach may seem appealing for several reasons. You will be buying a tried-and-tested system which someone else has already been using. In theory all the teething troubles should have been sorted out, and you will be able to work with something that does the job straight away.

However, there are a few caveats. It is important to remember that computer equipment depreciates quickly. This means that second-hand 'bargains' are rarely what they appear and, in many cases, you will be able to buy a new, much better system for the same price as a second-hand one.

31

Another problem is that for legal reasons software cannot usually be sold to a third party, even when it has been paid for in full by the original owner. This means you will not be eligible for any help the manufacturer may offer to users, and you will not be able to take advantage of any improved versions (upgrades) of the software that the manufacturer decides to release, unless you buy them at the full price.

Finally, you cannot be sure that someone else's system matches your needs. Their set-up may be perfect for them, but it may not be right for you.

Second-hand computer equipment does have its uses, though. If you are working to a very tight budget – a few hundred pounds, perhaps – then you will have to buy second-hand. In this part of the market the equipment has depreciated as much as it is going to, making it less of a long-term risk, but there are still pitfalls to watch for. The most worrying is that spare parts and consumables may no longer be available. Before buying, check that you can still get these for the second-hand machine. For example, some models of the Amstrad word-processor family of small computers use a special kind of plastic diskette to store information. These are no longer widely available. If you can find a source locally or perhaps buy up a large stock from somewhere else, you will find that these machines offer good value for simple word-processing and accounting tasks. Without a source of these consumables, however, they are only slightly more useful than a doorstop.

With a little help from your friends

In theory this is the best and cheapest way to get help. In practice, you should make absolutely sure that your friends and colleagues fully understand your computer requirements and have set up a similar system for themselves before you act on their advice. Unless you have a friend who is prepared to help you put a system together from start to finish, you should treat the advice of friends and colleagues as a source of useful, but not definitive, information.

FINANCING THE PURCHASE

You have three options:

- an outright purchase
- purchasing with a loan or other finance
- renting.

If you are buying for business purposes, each of these options will affect your cash flow and tax position in different ways.

Buying your computer outright

Buying a computer can represent a sizeable investment for a small business and buying one outright can jeopardise cash flow. However, you can claim this money back against tax as a 'writing-down allowance'. Currently this means the cost is spread over four years. After four years your computer is assumed to be worth nothing (unless you sell it) and you have claimed your initial outlay back against tax.

Computers can also be classified as 'short-life goods' with a separate writing-down allowance. If you sell your computer, you are allowed to offset the loss against tax instead of being taxed on the income from the sale. Because computer equipment depreciates so quickly this can make a significant difference to your tax liability, to the extent where the sale of an obsolete computer at nominal cost can sometimes be very worthwhile indeed.

Finance

Purchasing with finance can be a better deal, at least as far as short-term cash flow goes. You will usually need to put up some of the money yourself – banks and loan companies are not keen on 100 per cent loans, unless you are borrowing a lot less than you can afford – but you will be able to spread the cost over a much longer period.

Interest payments are also tax-deductible, so in effect you have the loan 'for free'. The capital value of the computer is depreciated in the usual way, and on top of this you simply add the interest from any payments you are making.

Renting

Renting is similar, with one important difference. All payments are immediately deductible as a direct business expense. Many renting schemes provide

the option of buying the machine outright at the end
of a set period – usually three or four years. The
sums charged are nominal and at the end of the
rental period it is possible that the computer is still
adequate for your needs. An outright purchase can
be a sensible option at this point. Rental payments
have been written off against tax, so with a single
modest payment you can purchase the computer.
This final payment can also be claimed as a capital
allowance.

One disadvantage of renting is that it can be much
more expensive. It is advisable to avoid short-term
rentals unless you need the equipment desperately.
Most business rental schemes work out significantly
more expensive than an equivalent loan repayment
system. However, the rental scheme covers you
against equipment failure and other problems, and
when you include these extra factors in the equation a
renting deal can become more appealing.

As ever, you should read the small print in the rental
contract to check the nature of the support that is
offered. If it meets your needs and is still cheaper than
an equivalent outright purchase then renting is more
advantageous for you than buying.

Most computer magazines carry advertisements for
rental computers. Several high-street stores operate
rental schemes. Radio Rentals, working with Olivetti,
has a rental scheme for home users which offers good
machines, with software, at reasonable prices.

While renting hardware may be a good idea, renting
software usually is not. Over the course of a few years
you may end up paying two or three times more to rent

35

software than to buy it outright. Some package deals include software at a fair price, and some companies ask for extra payment for software. In the latter case, it is worth shopping around to compare the price of buying the software.

PAINLESS BUYING

Now is the time to talk to each retailer and check the other services they offer, particularly technical support, warranties, money-back guarantees, delivery charges and delivery times. Confirm the quoted price. Make sure you get a price that includes VAT.

Haggling

If you are buying everything, including the software and a printer, from one supplier it can be worth trying to negotiate a lower price for the package. If the retailer is local and you can collect the goods in person, it can also be worth negotiating a price for cash. Some retailers, especially the smaller ones, prefer to take cash as it avoids cheque charges.

Don't be afraid to haggle. If your retailer refuses to reduce the price, try asking for essential extras (such as a couple of packets of floppy disks or a printer cable) to be thrown in for free. These are often low-margin items for retailers and they can comfortably afford to give them away in small quantities. At worst you will get a refusal. At best you can save yourself some money.

Smaller retailers may well ask you what the best price you heard elsewhere was. Some would rather have your business, even with wafer-thin margins, than lose your custom to a competitor. It is important to be honest here, because if you quote an unrealistic price the next question will often be 'And did they say they had them in stock and ready to go?'.

Special offers

Be wary of high-pressure 'special offer' deals. Some larger retailers will attempt to use sale techniques to close a sale, by implying that the offer will be available only for a limited period. Although very, very occasionally you may miss a genuine bargain, the general trend in the computer trade is for more power at a lower price – even six months can make a big difference. Unless you really want to order right away and have already decided on a particular retailer, then it is prudent simply to say that you will think about it.

Instructions

If you are a complete beginner, ask whether you will be sent any instructions on how to connect up your system before you place an order. A typical PC comes with five or six different items that need to be linked together, and it is not always obvious how this should be done. More thoughtful dealers include an instruction sheet or will be happy to talk you through the process over the phone. Remember to ask about this before you commit yourself to buying, as this kind of small extra can save you a lot of time later.

Ordering your computer

Confirm your order in writing, either through the post or by faxing it. For those buying by mail order many magazines offer pre-printed order forms that you can cut out and fill in, and then send or fax to your retailer as appropriate. It is important to keep a copy of this document, which is your proof that you purchased an item via the magazine. If your supplier goes out of business before your order is fulfilled and the magazine subscribes to the MOPS (Mail Order Protection Scheme) the magazine is then liable under MOPS to make up your losses.

If you need to have your order fulfilled quickly and have already discussed this with the retailer, make a note to that effect across the order – the suggested wording is 'to be delivered on [insert date here] as discussed with [insert salesperson's name here]. Time is of the essence in this contract.' If there are any problems and delivery is delayed this wording gives you the option of cancelling the contract.

Payment by credit card

The preferred method of payment is by credit card. If the retailer goes out of business the credit card company is liable for your loss as long as the cash price of the individual item you are buying is more than £100. There are exceptions to this rule: corporate credit cards and purchases made by anyone other than the named card-holder will not be covered by the credit card company. Transactions made from companies registered overseas should be covered as the major credit card issuers have agreed to meet these claims.

If paying by credit card, make sure that you will not be charged until the goods are despatched. It is not unheard of for companies to take an order for goods that are out of stock, take the money immediately and then fulfil the order a month or two later when the goods arrive in their warehouse.

Also check whether a credit-card surcharge will be added to your bill. Many smaller suppliers (and even a few larger ones) do this to offset the commission they have to pay the card company for each card-based transaction. Make sure you know where your supplier stands on this before telling him or her your card number.

Payment by debit card

Most retailers also now accept debit cards (for example, Switch, Delta). These give you no protection at all. Beware – some retailers will try to charge you a surcharge on these as well. Debit cards are not liable to the same surcharges as credit cards, they do not offer you the same degree of protection and they cost the retailer a fixed transaction fee, exactly like a normal cheque. If you have to pay by debit card (and this is not recommended unless you have no other option) make sure that you get an assurance that a credit surcharge will not be added to the bill. You may need to argue this point strongly. If your retailer insists on applying the surcharge, go elsewhere.

Payment by cash

If your retailer is local, you may prefer to pay by cash and pick up the goods yourself. This could save you the delivery charge (usually not more than £20 or so) and may give you the option of negotiating a better price.

If you decide to collect the goods yourself, ask if you can see your system working before you take it away. Apart from peace of mind, this also gives you a chance to see for yourself how to connect up the different parts of your computer. For a beginner this can be a major confidence-booster. It is also a chance to ask the support staff any simple technical questions.

Unfortunately only smaller retailers are able to provide this level of personal service. Some, although not all, larger companies tend to keep their sales and delivery teams well apart from their engineering and support staff. If you are dealing with one of these it is far more likely that you will be presented with a stack of boxes.

Paying on account

If you run a medium-sized business it can be worth trying to pay on account – 30-day terms are often possible if you can supply trading references. This offers all the usual advantages of improved cash flow, but these have to be offset against the amount of work you need to do to set up an account in the first place. If you are likely to be using a single retailer for most of your computer equipment purchases it can be advantageous to arrange an account facility.

Delivery

When the goods are delivered write 'Goods not yet inspected' on the consignment note. This improves your legal standing if you need to return the goods for any reason. Inspect your order as soon as possible and, if you have any queries, contact the salesperson responsible for your order immediately. Follow this up with written confirmation of any defects or missing items as soon as you can.

ADDITIONAL HIDDEN COSTS

The bulk of the cost of your computer system will come from your initial investment in hardware and software. By telephoning around and asking for quotes you should already have an idea of what these are likely to be, but there are other costs you also need to consider. The most important ones are listed below.

Consumables

If you are considering a laser printer, make sure you find out how many pages it prints before it needs new supplies. Then estimate how many pages you are likely to print. To get a realistic idea of how many you will print, double this number – at least. This allows for mistakes and misprints. Also check consumable costs.

Although ink-jet printers are cheaper, if you are printing in bulk the laser is typically one-third the cost of the ink-jet (comparing ink with toner).

Some printers use special paper, which is more expensive than ordinary paper. If you do a lot of printing, this would increase your running costs considerably. You will also need to budget for floppy disks to keep safety copies of your work and your software. Floppy disks can be expensive. It is cheaper to buy in bulk (100 or more) direct from specialist dealers, many of whom advertise in computer magazines. Buying disks in twos and threes from high-street computer, stationery and business stores is not cost-effective. For small quantities the high-street discount chains, such as Argos, offer a much better deal. Buying by the hundred may seem excessive, but it is easy to use this many by keeping regular backups. If you have arranged to make regular backups using some other medium, allow for these in your final budget.

Maintenance, training and support costs

How much is your maintenance cover going to cost? How much do you expect to pay for support? At the very least, you should allow for the purchase of books and magazines to help you get the best from your investment. At the other end of the scale you may opt for access to a full technical support line and a few training courses. These costs should be included in your budget before you buy.

Insurance

Are you going to insure your machine? Will your policy cover you for a replacement if it is damaged or stolen, or will you also insure yourself against loss of business if your computer becomes unavailable for any reason? You need to decide on just how vital your computer will be to your business, and how much you can afford to be without it – as well as how much you can afford to pay to cover yourself against this.

VAT and delivery charges

The prices of most computer equipment are quoted without VAT, so allow for this in your cash flow if you are VAT-registered, or simply write off the extra if you are not. You will probably also have to pay for the delivery of your system. This can add another £20 to the quoted price.

Telephone charges

If you are buying any on-line services, allow for their charges, and also for increased telephone-line use. Bills of over £100 a month are not unheard of but can usually be avoided with careful planning.

First, if most of your calls are long-distance, investigate switching to Mercury. You can also take advantage of various business deals and 'frequently called number' schemes to cut your costs even more.

Second, try to use the service during off-peak hours. It is possible to set up a system where the computer sends and receives mail and picks up news automatically during the early hours of the morning. Unless you need access to mail immediately, it's worth waiting till after the 6pm watershed.

And third, if you are expecting to spend a lot of time on-line, make sure you get the fastest modem you can. This can halve your costs and is well worth the small extra initial outlay.

Do not under-estimate the cost of consumables and other extras.

Software Decisions 3

A quick look through some computer magazines shows that most advertising concentrates on hardware. Computers are sold as boxes, rather than useful tools. The industry works on the basis that hardware is exciting, doubly so if it works faster than last year's hardware. Software, which is what turns the hardware into a useful tool, appears to be something of an afterthought.

Choosing the right software for the job

Software comes in two types. The first is the dedicated application, specialised for a single job: for example, an accounts package, which is designed to keep the books and cannot be used for anything else. To use this kind of software you just type in your information. All the setting-up has already been done for you.

The second is the general-purpose package, which gives you a framework in which to work. These have to be tailored to your needs before you can use them. In this group are all the large business software packages. A spreadsheet can be used not only for accounts but for tax, financial projections, balance sheets, and mortgage and loan calculations as well. Before you attempt any of these tasks, however, you

have to create a template for each one. This kind of software gives you two jobs instead of one – first you create a framework for the information, and then you add the information itself – but has the advantage that you can organise information to suit specific needs. However, setting up the software will take extra time.

The type of software you choose will depend on the kind of work you want to do. If you want a specific job done or if you are worried about the amount of time it will take you to master a computer, then a tailor-made package is a good choice.

If you would like to explore what a computer can do for you in a more general way and would prefer a more flexible approach, then one of the larger business packages such as Microsoft's Office Professional may suit your needs better. Some of these are very

46

powerful indeed, and there is often some overlap between the applications they include. For example, you could work out quarterly sales figures by geographical region using either a spreadsheet or a database. Neither type of software is 'right' for the job. You will simply approach the problem in two different ways, depending on which you use.

If you decide on the second type you will have the added advantage of integration. Large business packages are often designed to work with each other, so you will have the ability to move information from a database to a spreadsheet, and perhaps create some charts which could then be 'pasted' into a word-processor for a business report.

TRY BEFORE YOU BUY

It is important to avoid buying software without trying it out first unless you have absolutely no alternative. A 'try before you buy' approach can save time, temper and money in the long run. To a large extent, the software you choose determines whether you will be happy with your computer.

Training courses can be a good way to try out software before buying it. An alternative is to visit a dealer. This can present some problems, however, as few dealers and high-street stores will have the time or the inclination to demonstrate a software package in detail. In itself, this is useful as it can show you which dealers are prepared to be helpful. A dealer who is interested enough to discuss and demonstrate your software options is preferable to someone who resorts to high-pressure sales talk.

Magazine reviews can be another useful guide. Many magazines run multiple tests in which different products are compared with each other. Even if you do not understand them fully, you will get some idea of how well one piece of software rates against another. The best reviews include usability and productivity ratings, and use independent testers in work-related situations. These give an excellent indication of how easy it is to use a piece of software, and also how easy it is to get useful work done with it (the two are not always related).

Free offers

Free copies of trial software are often given away with computer magazines. Sometimes the software is fully functional, but not the latest version: a special offer inside the magazine lets you buy the current version at a reduced price. Alternatively, the software is a trial version which is limited in some way; it may be designed to work for a certain number of days, or a set number of times.

Older trial versions are an excellent way to try out software. As software dates far more slowly than hardware, you may find that an old version does everything you want it to. Unfortunately, manuals are not usually supplied with the software, although they may be available for a small charge from the manufacturer. Paying the extra also renders you eligible for free help from the manufacturer.

Limited-use trial versions allow you to try software for nothing. There are no notable drawbacks to this approach, and if you buy the full version it may be possible to keep the work you created using the limited one.

48

A variation of the trial version is the encrypted demonstration. This contains both a demonstration copy of the software that you can try out in the normal way, and a full working version which can be used only with a special access code. To obtain this code you telephone the manufacturers with your credit-card details and make a payment, they give you the code over the telephone and agree to send any manuals and other extras you need.

Be wary of this kind of offer. You may be tempted to make an impulse purchase. Test the software thoroughly before buying to be sure it really does meet your needs. You will pay the full recommended price for software bought this way, whereas by shopping around you can often get a sizeable discount on software.

Demonstration versions and money-back guarantees

Some business software vendors offer a 'no-quibble', money-back guarantee. You can try their software for a limited period (usually 30 days) and if you return it you get a full refund. This kind of approach gives you the opportunity to try out competing products at your leisure. Always ask if this kind of deal is on offer before you buy software.

Shareware

Shareware (often known slightly inaccurately as 'public domain') software is explicitly provided on a try-before-you-buy basis. The software is available for a nominal amount and comes with a legal agreement which states that it may be used for an evaluation period – typically 30 days – without payment. Once this time has elapsed the software must be either registered – you do this by sending a cheque to the author – or removed from your computer.

Most shareware is produced by independent software writers who work from home and do not have access to the development resources of a large company. The quality of such software can vary. The best shareware packages can compete with professional products costing many times the price, and for those on a very tight budget can be a cost-effective alternative to mainstream products. The worst examples are badly designed, hard to use and unreliable. Some professional products are also badly designed, hard to use and unreliable, but they are, as a rule, at least partially usable. Unfortunately this is not always the case with shareware.

There are two main sources of shareware: bulletin boards and public shareware libraries. Shareware libraries act as a clearing-house for shareware. They do not usually collect registrations but simply keep copies of many different shareware packages which are available for a small fee. The best produce comprehensive catalogues and maintain their own bulletin boards, which allow access to their stock of titles.

Freeware

A handful of software titles are freeware. As the name suggests they can be used by anyone for free. The author maintains the copyright, but the software can be legally copied and used by anyone. Freeware tends to be written by hobbyists or enthusiasts and is unlikely to offer much to the less experienced user.

DECIDING WHAT YOU WANT

Choose your software first and then find the hardware. This rule of thumb bears repetition. It is far more important to choose the right software than the right hardware as most reasonably priced hardware today can handle anything needed to run an office. If you work on this principle you are almost certain to get a smooth-running, efficient system that does what you want.

When buying a software package, watch for the following:

- **Ease of use** Does the package do what you want in a simple and straightforward way, or do you have to work around its quirks before you get results?
- **Features** Be wary of packages that claim to do everything. Some office-oriented software packages now come with so many options that a number of the features remain unused. Sometimes a cheap and basic package can be much better value – and prove more useful in everyday terms – than a more upmarket product. A spreadsheet, for example, is a good general-purpose tool for financial analysis, but if you want something to help with your accounts it may not be the ideal purchase.
- **Productivity** How much more easily and quickly will the software help you get your work done? (This is not quite the same as ease of use.) Some

51

packages are tricky and slow to set up, but once up and running are speedy and efficient. Others are easy to understand but can seem laboured once you have mastered the basics and are feeling more confident. The best software includes shortcuts and automation features for commonly repeated tasks. It also has on-line help – a brief summary of the manual within the program itself.

- **Hardware requirements** How much hard disk space does the package take up? How much memory does it need? How fast is it? Here again, modern software packages can be very demanding. A full installation of Microsoft's Office Professional system – a popular package which includes a word-processor, spreadsheet, business presentation generator and database – can take up over 60Mb of storage space. Competing packages from other major software companies make comparable demands. If you plan to install a number of applications, you will need to be sure that you can afford the hardware to cope with this.
- **Operating system requirements** Within the hardware specification you will find a reference to an operating system. Operating systems are a special kind of software that run your computer.

SOFTWARE BUYING TIPS

When buying software you should be very careful to make sure that it does what you want it to – in practice, as well as in theory. The most widely advertised business packages are office suites which include a word-processor, a spreadsheet, a database, a business presentation package and also extras such as a personal information manager or a home accounts program. These may seem appealing at first sight, especially as they are often sold at a discount, but they may not do exactly what you want. If all you want is some simple accounting tools to help with income tax and VAT, and a way of keeping track of your business contacts, you may well get better value from simpler and more specialised software.

Software is quoted with three prices. The first is the official retail price. The second is the 'competitive upgrade' price. This applies if you have a competing software product from another manufacturer: you trade in your old software and get new software in return. Some dealers will supply you with free software which qualifies for the upgrade deal, so you can buy from them at the reduced rate.

The third is the 'version upgrade' price. If you already own an older copy of the software, you can get a new copy – with improved features – by paying this price. The numbers and letters after the name of the software are important if you decide on this price level. For example, Word Pro v2.0 means you are buying version 2.0 of the Word Pro program (sometimes the 'v' is left out). The higher the number, the newer the software (hence, WordPerfect 6.0 is newer than WordPerfect 5.1). Version numbers are usually included in advertisements. By shopping around you can pick up one of these older versions at a bargain price and use it as the basis for an upgrade deal. Often you will pay less for the old version plus an upgrade than for the new package. You may find that the older version does the job you want and you will not need to upgrade.

VOUCHERS

With some upgrade deals, however, you may not get the software immediately. Instead, you will be given or sent a voucher which you then pass on to the manufacturer, sometimes with proof of ownership of relevant older or competing software. The software will arrive through the post. This can be irksome if you need to get on with some work quickly. Before ordering an upgrade of any kind, check to see if there are any vouchers involved and, if so, what the time scale will be. If you are going to have to wait for three weeks you may want to reconsider your purchase or factor this delay into your schedule.

BUNDLES

Another way to get cheap software is to accept a bundle that comes with your computer when you buy it. Many larger hardware dealers include an office suite as a bundle. If you do not want it, you can delete it or choose not to install it, but unless the software is what you want anyway you should be wary of allowing a bundle deal to sway your decision about where to buy. In practice, some bundles are not quite such good value as they appear.

DISKS AND MANUALS

If you do decide that a bundle is right for you, check that the disks and manuals are included.

Having a copy of the software on your hard disk is not enough. If something goes wrong and your hard disk loses the programs you have lost your software. You can of course make safety copies of your own but this can be extremely time-consuming. With manufacturer-supplied master disks this problem can be avoided. The software can be re-installed and work can continue as before (assuming that your information has also been backed up regularly). The same applies to the manuals. Although modern software often includes a help feature – in other words, help is included within the software itself – this can be sketchy. Access to printed manuals is essential for beginners and for reference.

Most dealers are willing to supply disks and manuals for an extra charge – a typical price might be around £80 for a full set of manuals and disks. Even with this extra cost you may find a bundle can save you money.

YEAR 2000 PROBLEM

Systems and software which use a date facility may not function properly after the end of the century. These systems use two digits instead of four for year calculations: for example, '1997' is shortened to '97'. This will cause problems in the year 2000 because many date calculations will be completely wrong – the computer will be unable to distinguish between 1900 and 2000. The Year 2000 problem is of most concern for big companies which use very large computer systems. It should not be a major worry for home users, unless they use, for example, accounting packages which are non-compliant, but because many systems are still being sold, as we go to press, which cannot cope with the century date change, it is important to ask when you buy a system or piece of software that may be affected whether it is 'year 2000 compliant'. Ask for written confirmation that it is, and do not buy anything that is not.

HARDWARE DECISIONS

From the outside, one computer looks very much like another. So why are some computers so much more expensive than others? How can you find the one that best meets your needs?

Several factors influence the selling price of a computer. Some, such as performance, can be measured objectively. Others, such as brand image, offer more elusive (some would say illusory) benefits. But for both beginners and professional users support stands out as being particularly important.

FACTORS TO CONSIDER

The following factors will affect the cost of a computer:

- **Speed** A computer's price is directly related to how quickly it can perform a task. For most office work an 'average' machine will be sufficient and the best value for money.

- **Space for your information** There is a limit to the amount of information a computer can store. As a rough guide the more your computer costs, the greater the limit. Unless you need to keep track of huge amounts of information, have to deal with thousands of clients' records or want to use your computer to work directly with sound or video then the space available in almost any modern machine will fit your needs.

- **Room to grow** Most modern computers can be upgraded to offer new facilities and better performance. This is easier to do on some machines than on others. Computer technology is improving all the time, and extras designed for the latest machines may not work with older ones. So if you buy an older computer you should assume that you will not be able to upgrade it, although in some cases it is possible.

- **Brand image** In theory you should get a better-quality product and better support from a large and established manufacturer than a smaller one. But a computer made by a large company with a famous name will cost more than one made by a small-scale start-up business. Brand image can be a red herring for the unwary buyer. Unless you are impressed by the products and support service of a big-name manufacturer, there is no good reason to go for the extra expense. A big name does not automatically guarantee you a better computer and may sometimes mean you are paying a lot for some fancy lettering on the case. However, it is more likely that a larger manufacturer will remain in business for the lifetime of the computer. And some of the larger companies, notably Dell and Compaq, do make an effort to provide high-quality support.

- **Support** The most important question to ask before buying is 'What happens if my computer goes wrong?'. You might expect the quality of after-sales service to be reflected in the price. This is not always true. Many buyers have found that they get better service from a small, locally based retailer who also sells hardware at a reasonable price. Small companies are sometimes run by enthusiasts who take the time to build up a good working relationship with their customers. A large company will often treat its customers more impersonally. It is advisable to find out about a dealer's support service before a problem occurs rather than after. Although there are no guarantees of support, you can check a dealer's attitude to it by asking a few questions.

WHAT'S INSIDE THE BOX?

By choosing your software first and making a note of the specifications required by that software you are on the way to ensuring that you get a system that will fit your needs.

However, some basic computer knowledge can also be useful. Here is a short introduction to the inside of a computer.

A computer consists of a main system unit with attached extras such as the keyboard, screen and printer. Inside the main system unit are the parts of the computer that do the actual work. They include:

- **Motherboard** This is the heart of the computer. It holds the processor chip that does the calculations, and also the RAM (random access memory) that the processor uses. The processor does all the work and the memory works rather like a desk in an office – it is used as a work area, where information can be held temporarily while being worked on.

- **Hard disk drive** (often shortened to hard drive, or hard disk) This provides fast-access, longer-term storage and is equivalent to a filing cabinet. Information held in the computer's memory is lost when it is turned off, so it has to be saved to the hard disk beforehand to make sure that it survives. It is loaded from the hard disk when it needs to be used.

- **Floppy disk drive** This is used to get information into and out of the computer. Software is often supplied as one or more floppy disks – small plastic wafers with a metal catch that protects a thin disk of magnetised plastic. The plastic holds the information and the rigid case protects it.

- **Memory**, hard disk and floppy disk capacities are all measured in megabytes (Mb). One megabyte is roughly equivalent to one million letters – including spaces and punctuation marks. You will also come across kilobyte (Kb – one-thousandth of a megabyte) and gigabyte (Gb – one thousand megabytes, occasionally shortened to 'gig') units of information capacity. A long letter might take up 3Kb, and an 80,000-word book might take up 700Kb. A large piece of software will need around 20Mb. Typical capacities are between 4Mb and 16Mb for a computer's main memory, 1.44Mb for a floppy disk drive, and 500Mb and upwards for a hard disk drive. Floppy disk drive capacities are more or less standard across all machines but the other figures can vary. Hard disk drive capacities are increasing rapidly.

- **Extras** are either internal and plug straight into expansion slots on the motherboard, or external, plugging into serial and parallel ports on the back of the machine. Expansion slots provide a direct connection to the computer's internals and allow you to add extra features, such as sound and graphics, by plugging them straight in. Most computers include blanking plates at the back to hide the slots when not in use.

- **Serial and parallel ports** are connectors on the back of the computer and are used to get information into and out of the machine in a less direct way. The printer is usually connected to the parallel port and the mouse (a small palm-shaped pointing device that is rolled around the desk) is connected to the serial port. (Parallel and serial refer to the way the information flows – either in big chunks or spread out along a single wire.)

IBM OR APPLE?

There are two kinds of computer that are widely available and they are sold in slightly different ways. Your choice will depend on the software you want to use. Businesses tend to use the common IBM-compatible standard (also known as a PC). Such machines are designed and built by a huge range of manufacturers and are available from all kinds of outlets, ranging from high-street stores to specialist dealers. The word 'compatible' means that all these machines are designed to work to the same specification. Hardware and software that work on one modern machine will work on all of them. (Note that this applies only to new designs. Old software will usually work in new machines, but the reverse is not true.) It is easy to exchange information between different brand names and models.

Design

Users with creative or artistic interests tend to favour computers made by Apple.

In general, Apple machines are much more popular with their users and inspire an almost religious devotion unmatched by other systems. Perhaps this is because Apple-compatible systems – both hardware and software – seem much more colourful and 'user-friendly' than their IBM counterparts. Apple hardware also tends to be more appealing aesthetically. However, the IBM market has the advantage of scale. Competition is very fierce within the PC market, and prices can and do fall spectacularly.

Light business

For home or light business use there is very little to choose between the two lines. The same kinds of software are widely available on both machines, and it is a case of trying out each brand to see which feels the most comfortable and easy to use.

Professional uses

For more serious and professional use, the markets diverge significantly. Apple machines are used more for applications such as design, and book and magazine publishing. Both the hardware and the software tend to be geared towards these areas of use. IBM machines are used for everything else. Equivalent 'creative' software is available, but powerful IBM machines tend to be used more for business-oriented applications. Prices diverge at this level too, with Apple machines becoming approximately half as expensive again as equivalently powerful IBM models – although this does not become a factor until the very top-line models in each range are compared. Apple machines tend to hold their resale value.

OTHER BRANDS

In terms of sales alone, IBM-compatibles and the various versions of the Apple Macintosh account for almost all of the market. There are other brands, however, most of which date from the early 1980s when the computer market was split between machines that were used for serious work and those that were used for games and entertainment. Although most of these are no longer available new, they are still widely available on the second-hand market.

The main disadvantage of these brands is a lack of service and support and the fact that they have become increasingly marginalised as the home-computer market has matured. IBM-compatibles and the Apple Mac are the industry standards, and information and soft-

63

ware are all widely available. Other brands therefore cannot be recommended except perhaps for someone who would like to dabble with computers without making a huge investment.

DESKTOP VS PORTABLE

You have one more choice to make when deciding on a specification, and that is whether or not to buy a portable computer. The advantages of a portable are obvious – you can use it anywhere, you can keep your important information with you all the time, and you can even use it to keep in touch with a larger computer at home or at the office.

There are disadvantages too: cost and security. Portables tend to be much more expensive than a desktop machine with a similar specification; you can pay £6,000 for a top-of-the-range model. As for ensuring the security of your information, you can install password protection on your portable, but anyone who is computer-literate can work around most password systems fairly quickly.

Battery life and weight are two further considerations. Only the very best portables offer more than a few hours of useful working time, so their range in the field is limited. Some portables are quite heavy: the shirt-pocket computer that can replace a desktop machine has not quite arrived yet.

Some people like the freedom of a portable, and if you can see yourself writing letters in bed before breakfast then a portable will be perfect for you. But for most ordinary office tasks a desktop machine will be cheaper, safer and easier to maintain and to use.

64

Portable computers

Portables come in a variety of shapes and sizes. The larger machines are now dated and almost obsolete; newer models are getting smaller and lighter each year. Within the portable family you will find the following kinds of machine.

Portables

'True' portables are still unwieldy, although they can be carried quite a distance. They tend to be large and bulky and are rapidly being superseded by more modern designs. Because many of these models are now obsolete they cannot be expanded in the way that more modern machines can. Battery life is poor and they are better suited to desk work than to use on

trains and planes. They do have batteries, however, so in theory they can be used anywhere.

Notebooks

Notebook machines are of a much more manageable size and weight. They are usually more or less A4 in size, but offer features which are similar to those found in desktop machines. All-in-one models which include extras such as printers, modems and CD-ROM drives within the one case are now available, although it is doubtful whether these are light enough to be easily carried a long way. Modern notebooks are expandable using the PCMCIA system and this allows tiny extras such as modems and soundcards – some of which are literally credit-card size – to be plugged into the case. Notebooks have become the portable standard since the early 1990s.

Sub-notebooks

These are even smaller versions of the standard notebook design. Sub-notebooks are an excellent choice for a general-purpose information manager and portable word-processing tool. They can be used for most of the tasks a desktop computer can do, but they are light enough to carry around with ease.

Electronic organisers and palmtop computers

At the bottom end of the market is the electronic organiser. This is an electronic version of the ring-bound personal organiser, comprising diary, address book and notebook, that was popular in the 1980s. Although slow compared with a well-specified desktop machine, electronic organisers can be useful tools. Larger electronic organisers are often known as palmtops. These are very simple, very cheap, full-function PCs in a handheld case. Most offer the following features:

- electronic notepad or word-processor
- electronic address book and phone number database
- electronic diary
- clock.

Most organisers can be linked to a desktop computer and information transferred between the two. This is an important facility – it means you can keep safety copies of your contacts on your main machine in case the organiser is lost or stolen.

All electronic organisers suffer from similar drawbacks: the keyboards and display windows are usually too small to be convenient. Most manufacturers resort to miniaturised keys in an attempt to work around this. Anyone used to typing on a full-sized keyboard may find it very hard to adapt.

In spite of this, electronic organisers can be a useful option if you cannot afford a full portable or if you need a handy portable address book and notepad.

Personal digital assistant

The personal digital assistant (PDA) is the next generation of portable computer products. The technology is in its infancy, and repeated customer surveys and magazine tests have shown that none of the current models is as useful or as usable as conventional organisers. As the technologies mature, however, it is likely that these will be the machines of the future. PDAs offer as an extra:

67

- handwriting recognition
- 'intelligent' features that attempt to second-guess what you are trying to do. For example, if you write in 'lunch' followed by a person's name, it will call up the diary section, enter a lunch date and perhaps include the other person's telephone number.

Buying tips

When buying a notebook you should remember to check with your dealer the level of support and service offered. Will the dealer's service scheme cover you if something goes wrong when you are on the road?

Check what software comes with the portable. A very useful extra is a data exchange program which enables you to transfer information to your main PC. On some machines this will need additional hardware. Other features to check for include:

- **Weight** How easy is it to carry the portable? Is it as portable and light as an organiser, or is it more 'luggable' and unwieldy?
- **Display quality** Try the computer out and look closely at the display. Watch out for mouse pointers that disappear when you move them, and for overall brightness and clarity. Will the display still be visible in bright sunlight? In general, TFT (thin film transistor) displays give the best results, but these are very expensive. (These displays are so good that some users fit a screen filter which low-

ers the viewing angle, so they can do confidential work in public.)

Both colour and monochrome displays are widely available. Most monochrome displays are actually 'greyscale', which means that a range of shades is possible, rather than plain black (or blue or green) and white. Colour is a useful extra, but not essential for most work.

- **How the mouse works** On portables, mouse pointers come in all shapes and sizes. Some manufacturers supply a standard mouse, although this can prove unwieldy for public use. The built-in track ball is the most convenient and should be placed in front of the keyboard, at the centre. Best of all, perhaps, is the trackpoint system, which uses a tiny plastic stub which sits between the G, B and H keys on the keyboard. Although small, this pointer system is very easy to use. Another good choice is the track pad – an area which is sensitive to finger pressure. As you slide your finger around the mouse pointer follows.

  If you are left-handed, you should also check where the mouse buttons are. On some models they are placed on the right-hand side of the keyboard; on the better designs they are in the centre.

- **Battery life** You can expect a couple of hours of use from nickel cadmium (NiCad) batteries, maybe twice that from NiMH (nickel magnesium hydride) -type batteries. Lithium ion designs are the latest development and promise improved power capacity in a smaller and lighter package.

69

Check whether any spare batteries are included. These can be a useful, if expensive, extra which allow you to keep working for longer without access to a power source. The best portables allow batteries (and other extras) to be 'hot-swapped' – plugged in and out without turning the machine off. International compatibility is also worth watching for – will your portable work directly off the mains supply of another country?

It is advisable to check power-management options and power-down features. Some machines include a very useful 'sleep' mode, which lets you carry on working from exactly where you were when you turned the machine off. Others need to be powered down more deliberately if you want to keep your work.

Power management features range from simple battery meters to optional power-saving modes which will temporarily power down a hard disk if it is not used for a set time.

- **External connectors** On some machines a floppy disk drive is an optional and external extra. If you have a connection to a desktop machine, you may not find this is a problem. But if your portable is your only computer you will need some way to get software into it and information out of it. Check whether a floppy disk drive is included, and whether or not it is built into the machine.

You should check also whether or not you can connect to a printer. Some machines, especially those built for docking stations, do not let you do this directly.

On IBM-compatible portables check the number and type of PCMCIA slots. If you need a modem and a soundcard, for example, check that the portable has room for these extras. You should also check the available memory. 4Mb is the minimum for an older Windows-compatible machine, while 8Mb is required for Windows 95. If you are using an older model with 2Mb or less then you should ask whether an upgrade is possible, and if so how much it will add to the price.

- **Infra red links** The very latest organisers include an IR information transfer system. This makes it easy to exchange information with other organisers and suitably equipped PCs.

OBSOLETE BARGAINS

You will see computers advertised for less than £500. Many of them are machines that are now obsolete and being sold as bargains. Depending on what you want from your computer, these can offer good value. However, modern machines can be upgraded to make them more powerful and therefore a better investment in the long run, as their effective working life is extended and they can be made to work with more modern and powerful software tools. This will not apply to an obsolete machine. It will be harder to upgrade, will not work with modern software and, eventually, it may even need to be sold or thrown away completely.

However, in practice this may not be a problem. For simple, undemanding tasks a cheap obsolete machine may be perfect, as long as you buy it knowing its limitations. If you cannot envisage your computer needs expanding significantly in the near future, then an older machine can be a good buy. Bear in mind that if it is very old you should check for the availability of consumables in the same way that you would for a second-hand machine.

UPGRADES

All recent computers can be upgraded to take advantage of new technology as it becomes more widely available. If you buy a reasonably priced computer – costing around £1,000 or so – you will almost certainly find you have a range of upgrade options to choose from.

When starting out, however, it is prudent to ignore these until you are familiar with your machine and have got the most you can out of it. If you have an older machine you may find yourself under pressure from trade magazines (perhaps even from friends) to bring it up to more modern standards. Think long and hard before you do. If your computer serves all your current needs, there is no reason for you to upgrade. You should only start to think about this seriously if you feel that your machine is annoyingly sluggish at times, or if some new software arrives which could be useful to you but will not work on your machine.

In general, it can be worth buying a slightly more powerful machine than you need. For office work, however, it is unlikely that a working system will need to be updated more than once every few years at most. This corresponds to the time it takes a generation of computers to move down from the leading edge to

72

obsolescence. In a business context, it also corresponds to the four-year writing-down period for capital tax allowances. It is not usually advantageous to get a cheap machine with a view to upgrading later.

The situation is slightly different for home computers that are used for playing games as well as for work. Surprisingly, perhaps, games are much more demanding of computer power than most office applications. You will find that a computer used for games has a much shorter active life and will also need to be upgraded regularly. If games are a serious interest then consider buying the very best computer you can afford.

BUYING STEP BY STEP

By choosing your software first, you have already decided on the hardware to make it work. Most software comes with a minimum, or a typical, hardware specification which is mentioned somewhere on the packaging or in the manual. You can quote this directly to a dealer, even if you do not understand what the words mean. Where possible, choose a 'typical' or 'recommended' rather than a 'minimum' specification, as these will give you the extra power to work comfortably. By following the specifications you will get a computer that does what you want, rather than the one the dealer wants to sell you. What you choose depends on your requirements. If you foresee your needs expanding, choose a better and more powerful machine than the software specification suggests. If you are looking for a system for basic office work that you can install and forget, ignore the high-pressure sales techniques and follow the specifications.

73

Contacting local dealers

Once you have a rough specification, you can start contacting a few dealers. The best place to look first is in your local *Yellow Pages*. Quote the specification you need, explain which software you will be using, mention that you are a beginner and will need good support, and see what kind of response you get. If you find someone sympathetic and helpful, ask if he or she can do a package deal which includes all the software you want.

In any conversation with a dealer, note down the time and date, the name of the person to whom you spoke, and any prices you are quoted. You can leave any further details, such as warranties and extras, for a later call. Make a list of the dealers who seem knowledgeable and approachable, together with their best quoted prices. If you find a dealer who responds positively on the telephone, it is worth making a visit to see how you are treated in person. Do not be surprised if you find yourself in a shabby-looking shop instead of a stylish showroom; it is the level of enthusiasm, interest and professionalism which is important.

Contacting nationwide dealers

Your next step is to repeat the exercise with dealers from further afield. You will find these advertised in any computer magazine. Buying long-distance has its drawbacks, but finding out the going rate for hardware on a nationwide basis can sometimes give you a good negotiating position with your local dealer.

The advantage of buying from a larger company – such as Dell or Gateway – is that they are more likely to be financially stable and less likely to disappear overnight. The disadvantage is that they will often charge you more for their services.

Smaller dealers usually offer slightly better prices. Some machines are assembled in garages and bedrooms, advertised in the low-cost trade weeklies and sold by mail order. Others are built by huge companies with multi-million-pound turnover. Both kinds of dealer use the same sets of parts, which are bought in bulk from wholesale electronic design companies in South East Asia. The only thing that distinguishes these wares is the level of support the dealers can offer you, and the care and attention the manufacturers give to assembling their machines.

Advertising ploys

Smaller dealers sometimes quote rock-bottom prices and it is not until you read the small print that you discover that the system is incomplete – a keyboard, screen and mouse are extra. Another tactic is to sell the operating system (DOS, and/or Windows) as an 'optional' extra. This can add about £70 to the quoted price. To get round this you should ask whether the price you have been quoted includes everything you need to run your software right away. Then, just to be sure, check if there are any 'extras' you need. As usual, you should make a note of the replies.

LOOKING AFTER YOUR COMPUTER

Before you buy your computer, you need to be sure that you are protected from the various things that can go wrong. Computers can and do break down. They can also be stolen or damaged. Sometimes the problems are easy to fix and no harm is done apart from a few hours' delay. At other times the results can be catastrophic, with months or even years of work obliterated in seconds. How can you protect yourself? And what other dangers do you need to take into account?

WARRANTIES

As a first step, it is essential to make sure you get a warranty with your computer.

Back-to-base warranties

The simplest is the back-to-base warranty. Under this scheme your computer will be repaired, and defective parts replaced, if, and only if, you send the computer back to the retailer. You pay the cost of this initial delivery, although the retailer usually pays for the return of your machine.

This is the standard minimum warranty you will be offered. It has very serious limitations if you are planning to rely on your machine for business purposes. First, the warranty is worth nothing unless you can return the machine to where you bought it. If your retailer is not local you can expect to pay between £10 and £15 for a next-day delivery using a courier service.

Second and far more important, this kind of warranty does not usually guarantee how quickly your machine will be repaired. If it needs to be sent back to the manufacturer it may take weeks. If you rely on your computer on a daily basis this kind of delay can be extremely inconvenient.

Reputable dealers may be willing to provide you with a temporary machine while the repairs are being done. This is a useful option to have, but bear in mind that when your computer goes back to the manufacturer, so does all the information – including the software – you keep on it. Even if you keep safety copies of your work, recreating your working environment on a new machine can take anything from an evening to a few days.

Collect-and-return warranties

A variation on the back-to-base warranty is known as collect-and-return. Although once popular, it is now becoming increasingly rare. With this warranty you do not have to pay carriage costs. This is a slightly better option, but all the same caveats apply.

On-site warranties

Far more useful is the on-site warranty. Under this scheme your supplier contracts to send an engineer to you when something goes wrong. Unfortunately, it is still no guarantee that your computer will be repaired immediately.

On-site warranties vary greatly. Sometimes they are available as an optional extra when you buy a machine. You may even get one year's free on-site service as part of the initial purchase deal, and another year or two for an extra fee. However the deal is arranged, it is advisable to check the small print of the service contract. Watch out for the following:

- **Call-out time** A warranty that guarantees that your computer will be looked at within eight hours of your call is worth much more to you than one that states that it will be repaired within five working days.
- **Charges** What exactly does the warranty cover – parts, labour, both or neither? Is there any kind of excess charge for the first part of any costs?
- **Company reputation** Many dealers subcontract their warranties to independent support firms, some of which are reliable and professional; others are cowboys. Try to get the telephone number of the support company from your dealer. Then telephone the support company and ask about its charges, call-out times and references from customers. The quality, tone and efficiency of the answers will indicate the kind of support you can expect. If you like the way the company works, take the opportunity to ask about its services. You may even want to think about taking out a longer-term contract.
- **Company stability** The worst possible situation to find yourself in is with a warranty contract from a

company that has gone out of business. This happens a lot and the upshot can vary from inconvenient to disastrous.

- **Experience and references** Does the company know what it is doing? Some firms have been known to claim to maintain certain types of computer when in fact they have no experience of them at all. If in doubt, ask for references. Experienced and reputable companies will be able to provide these.
- **Resources** Ask about the company's 'back-room' technical resources and repair facilities. Does it subcontract the work?
- **Contract** Ask to see a standard warranty contract in advance. If your request is refused, be very wary.
- **Location** The company should be within easy travelling distance or have a local office.
- **Quality control** Is the company certified as complying with the ISO 9000 or older BS5750 quality-control standards? Or is it applying for certification? These impressive-sounding titles guarantee the existence of quality-control procedures, but offer no further assurance that work really is done to high standards. In practice, the certification system seems to be open to potential abuse, and some quality-control professionals are unhappy with the loopholes that exist. It is likely that these standards will be changed soon. In the meantime, it is wiser to judge a company's reliability on the other criteria mentioned here.

79

Finally, with on-site warranties, you should also check that the warranty covers **printers and monitors** as well as the computer itself.

INSURANCE

An increasingly popular option for some businesses is to take out insurance. This pays for the cost of any repairs and may also help indemnify your business against problems caused by the loss of your computer.

Getting insurance for a computer used at home can be problematic. If you run an office from home, insurers are likely to consider your computer a business asset and will be unwilling to insure it under a normal home and contents policy. Some companies will insure you, but only if you meet certain conditions – for example, if you receive very few business visitors.

Home office policies

Special home office policies are available. Some of these provide you with the equivalent of a maintenance contract, and some insurance policies compare favourably with maintenance arrangements. You should investigate both types of policy to give yourself the widest range of options. Others are fully comprehensive policies which cover you against damage by water, fire, theft, and may even include extra funds which allow you to hire a machine while your original computer is being repaired. A number of policies also include options which cover the costs of 'reinstating' data, which can mean recompiling it from the original sources, or paying someone else to do this for you.

Some will even cover you for 'consequential loss', although this is usually an expensive option. This means that if you lose work because your computer is out of action, you will be reimbursed for some or all of your financial losses.

Small print

As with any insurance policy, it is a good idea to read the small print to see what conditions you have to fulfil for the policy to be valid. You will normally be charged an excess – typically £50 – if you make any claim. Some policies also stipulate certain security arrangements you need to take to minimise your risks. These vary from making sure that data is safe, by keeping safety copies and checking for viruses, to making your premises as theft-proof as possible – perhaps bolting your computer to your desk. If you work in an 'unsafe' environment, expect to pay extra. Most British policies cover the use of notebook computers in the UK, but if you travel abroad a lot you will usually be asked to pay extra.

BACKUPS

Even without insurance, you can take steps to make sure that your information is as safe as possible. This is vital, especially for business use. Your first step is to save your work regularly on the computer's hard disk. If something happens it will still be

81

there when you turn on the machine again. Some software has an auto-save feature which does this automatically.

Once your information is on disk, you need to make copies and keep them somewhere safe. These are known as backups, and are a time-consuming but essential chore.

Floppy disks

These are ideal for low-volume work. You can simply copy the information from the computer to a floppy disk. 50Mb is about the maximum you can comfortably archive on floppy disks. (This is how the backup copies of this book were maintained – the text fits on to a single 1.44Mb high-density disk.) Most computers come with a free backup utility that packs the information more tightly on to each disk and also automates the process across multiple disks. As a rough guide, you can expect to spend about 20 minutes archiving 50Mb of information.

QIC tape streamers

For higher volume work, the cheapest option are QIC (quarter-inch-cartridge) tape streamers. These use small tape cassettes to store large amounts of information – 250Mb, 400Mb and 750Mb are typical sizes. The units are fairly cheap – about £200 for a 750Mb system. They are slow but can be left running overnight unattended unlike a floppy disk-based system. The cartridges themselves are also cheap – around £15 for a 250Mb cartridge.

Tape cartridges do not have a reputation for reliability. Where possible you should verify information after you have backed it up to confirm that it has been recorded accurately. Backup software is usually supplied with the tape streamer. You should make sure that it includes a 'verify' option.

DAT systems

Digital audio tape systems are more reliable, but also much more expensive. At the time of writing DAT systems cost around £700, and offer 2Gb of storage – ample for most situations. The system also uses tape cartridges, but these are much smaller – half the size of an audio cassette – and much more robust. A DAT system is recommended if you need a 'bullet-proof' backup system.

Tape-based systems suffer from the disadvantage of being linear – the information is arranged in order along the tape. If you want to restore some information that is at the end of the tape, you have to wait for the tape to wind to the right position. A tape system is recommended if you do full backups of everything on a regular basis, which you should do at least once a month, ideally once a week. It is also possible to do incremental backups. These only backup the information that has changed since the last full backup. This should be done daily.

Tape backup systems also suffer from more subtle drawbacks. Tape wear can be a problem if you use the system regularly, and this can lead to wasted time if you regularly have to back up the backups to prevent information loss. Another problem is print-through – information tends to leach to adjacent loops of tape when the tape is tightly wound. In large organisations which maintain huge tape archives, these are regularly unwound and retensioned to minimise this problem.

CD-R

One final backup option is CD-R – you create a CD with your own information written on it. These special writable CDs are as reliable and robust as any other CD and offer a high capacity – around 650Mb. Disk blanks cost around £15 – much less in bulk. At around £1,300 this is currently the most expensive option, but prices are likely to fall sharply over the next few years. In fact by the end of the century it is likely that this will be the backup standard – and perhaps even the information exchange standard – used on most machines.

SOFTWARE BACKUPS

As well as keeping your information safe, it is a very good idea to make safety copies of the software you use. If it is supplied on floppy disks, you should make copies and never use the originals. You will need between 50 and 100 floppy disks to make a backup of a typical full set of business software. Although it is a tedious chore, the advantages of this single task outweigh the disadvantages. If your hard disk loses its information and your software originals have

84

become defective, you will have to buy the software again – even if it is one disk out of ten that is at fault. Making safety copies can save you time and temper later.

Storing backups

All backup copies should be stored somewhere safe and secure. The ideal is a fire-proof safe, or perhaps, if the information is sensitive as well as valuable, a bank safety-deposit box. A cheaper option is simply to keep safety copies somewhere off the premises – perhaps at home, or at a friend's or relative's house. If your business premises are burgled or burn down, your safety copies will still be intact.

VIRUSES

Computer viruses are simple programs that hide among useful information and then copy themselves into your computer. Once there, they copy themselves on to any disks you use. If you swap information with a colleague's machine then that computer will also become 'infected'. Software received over the telephone can also pass on the virus.

Some viruses are harmless, others are irritating and little more than elaborate practical jokes. A handful are devastating and can wipe out all the information inside your machine. Without special tools it is impossible to check whether or not your computer is infected or to do anything about it. Fortunately, these tools are readily available, easy to use and affordable.

85

It is possible to protect yourself from viruses by following a few simple rules. Never swap information with anyone unless you have to. When exchanging information electronically, only software can infect your machine. Text, graphics, sound clips and electronic mail messages are all virus-free. If you transfer any software over the telephone, check for viruses before using it.

If you need to work with other people's floppy disks, anti-virus software is recommended. This removes existing viruses and keeps new viruses out of your machine. Anti-virus packages respond only to viruses that have already been isolated and analysed. New viruses are being created all the time. Many packages now include a subscription option that will keep you safe from the latest examples.

COMPUTER SECURITY SYSTEMS

If you work with other people, you may need to make sure that your private information remains private. Short of encrypting information, there is very little you can do to prevent a computer expert from gaining access to your computer. Desktop computers simply are not secure, and most security systems have loopholes.

BIOS passwords

On PCs, the most secure option you have is to use a BIOS password which you type in when the machine is starting up. This can only be changed by opening the case and short-circuiting or removing the battery on the main computer board. There is no easier way to change it if you forget it. Unfortunately, not all PCs have this option. Check with your dealer if security is important to you.

Screensaver passwords

For less secure applications, you can use a screensaver password. Most screensavers include a password feature which locks your machine so it cannot be accessed if you leave your desk. (A BIOS password offers protection only while the machine is starting up. Once it is running there is nothing to prevent anyone getting access to your records.) Password protection is perhaps the most useful feature of a screensaver. The protection can easily be 'hacked' by an expert, but it will deter casual users from trying to access your machine.

Many networks include reliable security features, most of which are password-based. If you forget your password, your network supervisor will be able to create a new one for you.

Problems with passwords

All password systems can be fallible if the password is obvious, or obviously visible. Never use a password that can be guessed easily such as the names of friends, children or spouses, or words associated with your hobbies. PIN numbers are another bad choice. The best passwords are nonsense combinations of words and letters which are all but unguessable.

87

Avoid typing in your password if anyone is standing close by. Never write a password down, but if you have to, don't keep it anywhere near the computer itself. It is traditional in some businesses to keep passwords on sticky notes under the desk or in a drawer or as a note in an address book. Avoid all of these options. Finally, change your password regularly – at least once a month, preferably once a week, perhaps even once a day if security is very important to you.

Some security systems are hardware-based. The most common of these is the floppy disk lock, a disk-sized square of plastic that can be locked into the floppy disk slot with a key. Disk locks are a good way to avoid viruses and unauthorised copying of software, but they will not protect you against unauthorised access to your computer.

PREVENTING COMPUTER THEFT

Many insurance companies will ask you to improve security before they will agree to give you a policy. They will consider loss-of-earnings policies for home and business users, but may start to insist you secure your premises. The theft losses have been quite staggering. Some insurers used to do a flat rate, but now include location-based payments. Premiums can vary by as much as 400 per cent between safe and high-risk areas.

- Look for a **good standard of security generally**. The first step is to keep the burglars out. That means curtains and blinds to hide the equipment so it can't be seen from outside, as well as reliable locks.

- **Internal security is important**. Who is doing the cleaning, for example. If it is contracted out, who are the contractors using? Are they trustworthy, or are they likely to leave the key with someone? Laptops are another problem. Some thieves just walk in in broad daylight and help themselves to anything that is not watched or secured.
- Once the burglar is in a **building with an alarm system** he needs to work fast. The police can get to an alarm in under ten minutes, but it is important that the keyholder is on hand to let them in. Sometimes this can take an hour or more, by which time it is too late to do anything. If the criminals can get in without an alarm, they will spend all night taking things apart. Now that lock-down plates are common, some gangs

89

are taking computers apart and just stealing the chips.

- **Property marking** is another useful deterrent. It makes it harder to resell things. Big organisations such as health and education authorities are going down the route of overtly marking everything very clearly. It is easy to change the case on a PC so it is not so important there, but with Macs it is harder and marking is more of a deterrent.

- For software and work, **backups are essential**. Some businesses fold when they lose everything because they have not protected their work. Boxed sets with the original packaging are very appealing to thieves. They can be sold at car boot sales, so take the software out of the boxes and throw them away.

- If you take serial and model numbers, get rid of attractive packaging, anchor the hardware, reinforce the doors, put in an alarm and make regular backups you are as safe as you can be. But the police still like to go to individual premises, so you should **call in your crime prevention officer** – the advice is free – preferably before it happens.

Many insurance companies will ask you to improve security before they will agree to give you a policy. They will consider loss-of-earnings policies for home and business users, but may start to insist you secure your premises. The theft losses have been quite staggering. Some insurers used to do a flat rate, but now are including location-based payments. Premiums can vary by as much as 400 per cent between safe and high-risk areas.

Travelling with your portable computer

- Make sure your computer is insured
- Back up your information before you leave
- Put a BIOS–based password on your system
- Mark your name, address and phone number on your portable
- Remember to charge up the battery before you leave in case you are asked by airport security to turn it on. Also bring your AC plug to recharge the battery for the return journey
- Keep a floppy disk inside the drive so that dirt or small objects do not get into it
- Put sensitive information on a diskette, or if your hard drive is removable take it out and keep it separate from the computer when you are not using it
- Always carry the computer as hand luggage
- Do not carry a floppy disk through the metal detector as it will be erased or corrupted
- Do not put your computer on the conveyor belt. Ask for it to be hand-checked instead. The radiation exposure will damage the battery
- Keep your portable in the centre of a soft bag so that it is protected, easy to get at and not obviously a computer
- Do not keep the computer in the overhead compartment of an aeroplane. The disk can be damaged or erased if it is kept near a speaker
- Do not use your portable during the first and last ten minutes of a flight.

INDEX

Here's just a flavour of some of the reports planned for future issues of *Which?*

• Multimedia PCs on test • Tumble driers • Stereo systems • Compact cameras • Current accounts • Claiming on car insurance • Health insurance • Shopping on the Internet • Washing machines • Large family cars • Postal deliveries • Council Tax • Package holidays • Credit reference agencies • Best Buy PEPs

---

So why not take up our trial offer today?

── SUMMARY OF OFFER ──

3 free issues of Which? as they are published • Just fill in the delayed direct debiting instruction below and post it to Which?, FREEPOST, Hertford X, SG14 1YB • If you do not wish to continue beyond the free trial period simply write to us at the address above, and to your Bank/Building Society to cancel your direct debiting instruction, before the 1st payment is due • You first payment will be due on the 1st of the month 3 months after the date you sign the mandate (so for example, if you sign the mandate on 15th August, your 1st payment is due on 1st November) • No action is necessary if you wish to continue after the free trial. We will send you Which? each month for the current price of £14.75 a quarter, until you cancel or until we advise you of a change in price • We would give you at least 6 weeks notice in advance of any change in price, so you would have plenty of time to decide whether to continue — you are of course free to cancel at any time.

Offer subject to acceptance. Which? Ltd, Reg in England Reg No 677665. Reg Office 2 Marylebone Road, London NW1 4DF. Reg under the Data Protection Act. As result of responding to this offer, your name and address might be added to a mailing list. This could be used by ourselves (Which? Ltd, or our parent company Consumers' Association) or other companies for sending you offers in the future. If you prefer not to receive such offers, please write to Dept DNP3 at the above Hertford address or tick the box on the coupon if you only want to stop offers from other companies. You will not be sent any future offers for 5 years, in compliance with the British Code of Advertising and Sales Promotion.

--- --- --- ── ▼ DETACH HERE ▼ ── --- --- ---

Your name and address in BLOCK CAPITALS PLEASE

Name (Mr/Mrs/Miss/Ms)	Address
	Postcode

To: Which?, FREEPOST, Hertford X, SG14 1YB
Please send me the next 3 months' issues of Which? magazine as they appear. I understand that I am under no obligation – if I do not wish to continue after the 3 months' free trial, I can cancel my order before my first payment is due on the 1st of the month 3 months after the date I sign the mandate. But if I decide to continue I need do nothing – my subscription will bring me monthly Which? for the current price of £14.75 a quarter.

Direct Debiting Instruction Please pay Which? Ltd Direct Debits from the account detailed on this Instruction subject to the safeguards assured by The Direct Debit Guarantee. I understand that this Instruction may remain with Which? and if so, details will be passed electronically to any bank or building society.

Signed	Date

Bank/Building Society account in the name of	Name and address of your Bank/Building Society in BLOCK CAPITALS PLEASE

*Banks/Building Societies may decline to accept Direct Debits to certain types of account other than current accounts

To:

Bank/Building Society Acct. No.

☐☐☐☐☐☐☐☐

Tick here if you do not wish to receive promotional mailings from other companies ☐

Bank/Building Society Sort Code

☐☐ – ☐☐ – ☐☐

Postcode

── **NO STAMP NEEDED • SEND NO MONEY** ──